THE APPLIQUÉ QUILT

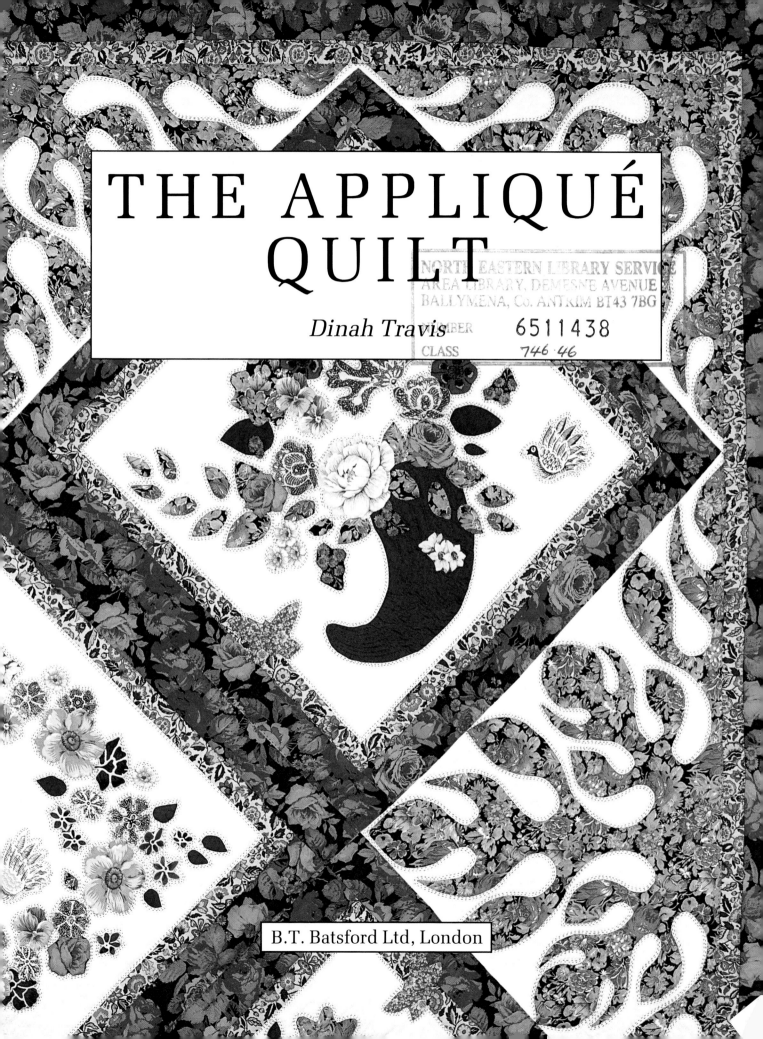

THE APPLIQUÉ QUILT

Dinah Travis

B.T. Batsford Ltd, London

First published 1993
© Dinah Travis 1993

Typeset by Goodfellow & Egan
Phototypesetting, Cambridge
and printed in Singapore

Published by
B.T. Batsford Ltd
4 Fitzhardinge Street
London W1H 0AH

British Library Cataloguing-in-Publication data.
A catalogue record for this book is
available from the British Library.

ISBN 0 7134 7035 6

Jacket illustration
Rondo quilt by the author

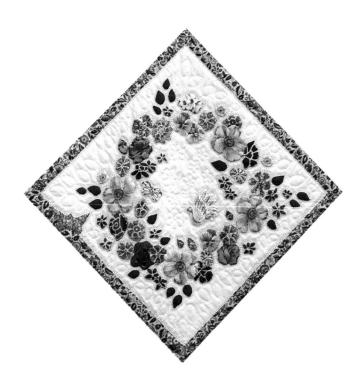

CONTENTS

ACKNOWLEDGEMENTS

I would like to express my thanks to my colleague Pat Salt for all her support in developing the course on which this book is based and for the many hours spent together sorting through possible creative teaching ideas to suit both diffident and experienced quilters, for then reading the original text for technical detail and for allowing me to use photographs of her work. Thanks also to my husband for always being ready to discuss the book at any time and for reading through the proofs with me. I would also like to thank the students of Bromley Adult Education for their enthusiastic support in the way that they are prepared to take on new ideas in designing and making quilts and for allowing me to use photographs of their quilts in this book. Finally, thanks again to the Batsford staff for their help and understanding.

Introduction

What is appliqué? The dictionary defines appliqué as work cut out from one material and affixed to the surface of another. So in patchwork terms, appliqué is shapes cut out of one fabric and sewn on to another fabric.

There are examples of appliqué on coverlets and quilts dating from the early eighteenth century, and perhaps even earlier, to the present day. Some of these are fairly sophisticated in the use of pre-printed designs; others are naïve folk cut-outs of simple, everyday scenes. The main consideration when designing a piece of appliqué work is the arrangement of shapes within a blank space. Most of us feel safe in placing an important shape centrally and subsidiary ones symmetrically around it, but give little thought to the shapes made in the background by placing one shape within another.

In this book I hope to encourage you to find and use the whole space of your quilt, while at the same time enjoying the freedom that appliqué gives you to choose and express your own ideas in a positive way. I plan to do this by showing straightforward and often simple methods of creating your own shapes, together with colour drawings which demonstrate the possibilities of using these methods within a quilt design. The best way to approach a design is not to think 'I can't draw', but to relax and think more constructively about the problem. Often it is a lack of practice in drawing since we were at school, and even then we were perhaps told that we had no talent. Think of drawing as a means of note-taking for your own personal use, not as something to be displayed publicly. We all makes notes in some form or other, even if it is only a shopping list.

In the book I have described different ways in which you can apply one piece of fabric to another, and different ways in which you can construct a quilt. I do not design a quilt for you, but give you the means to design the quilt you would like in your own individual style and to your own measurements.

***Rondo** quilt by the author, showing blocks of a wreath, a cornucopia, a basket, a bowl and a bunch of flowers surrounded by a folded cut-out border of leaf shapes*

1
Requirements

The main requisite for making a quilt is a love of fabric and pattern. It is also helpful to have an urge to create something with fabric, whether it be large or small: it could be a king-sized bed quilt or a small wallhanging that you make.

Quilts can be made quite economically from a rag-bag of scrap fabrics, or fabrics can be bought and co-ordinated especially for the job. A quilt made from family scraps will have a dimension all of its own with lots of memories, while a quilt made from co-ordinating fabrics bought in the high street will certainly not be unique in the same way. Search around at home, ask friends and hunt in the sales and at your local market, as well as in the large city stores and in mail-order catalogues, for unusual fabrics that will make your quilt into something special.

The appliqué quilts in this book can be made from the simplest of equipment and materials — there is no need to go out and spend a large amount of money on the latest fashion in fabrics or fancy gadgets. Over the centuries quilts have often been made in the very poorest of home circumstances.

A quilt can be made from the following simple list:

- the usual sewing tools: needles, sewing thread, pins, a thimble and scissors
- a table to work at and to lay the work out on
- an iron and ironing-board
- a supply of paper and card easily cut with scissors
- basic drawing tools: a pencil, ruler, eraser and scissors for cutting card and paper (these should be kept separate from those used to cut fabric)
- a supply of cotton fabrics
- a place in which you can hang the pieces of the quilt for viewing during progress
- a large, flat area where the completed quilt can be laid out and admired
- a sewing machine, although this is not essential for this type of quilt

You will know instinctively what is required based on your own experience of sewing, and will adjust to any new needs which may occur while making the quilt.

Quilt by Pat Salt showing wreaths, bowls, bows and baskets of flowers on a striking black background. Some of the roses have been stencilled by Pat to fit in with ready-printed ones and applied using the **broderie perse** *technique (see page 24)*

2
Tools and materials

It is a good idea to have ready at hand good tools that are fit for the job. There is nothing complicated about basic drawing and sewing tools, but it is easier to achieve a good result with the right equipment.

Drawing tools

You will need drawing equipment to help in drawing out plans, in making templates and for designing the quilt.

Rulers are essential for drawing good straight lines: a metre (or yard) rule for extra-long lines, a 30 cm (12 in) rule for general work and a 15 cm (6 in) rule for short, intricate lines. These three sizes will deal with any straight lines that may need drawing while you are designing the quilt.

A protractor is useful to help in drawing unusual angles and to check the accuracy of right-angles.

A pair of compasses is needed to draw circles of a prescribed size, and for use in constructing and dividing angles.

A plastic eraser is useful for rubbing out mistakenly drawn lines, not only on paper but also on fabric.

A hard (H) pencil is used to draw accurately when size is absolutely essential. The higher the number, the harder the lead. Always keep the pencil sharp whatever is being drawn. I generally use a 3H for this type of drawing.

A soft (B) pencil makes a mark more easily on paper or fabric than a hard pencil. The higher the number, the softer the lead, and the freer it is to draw or express a line. I generally use a 2B pencil for design work.

Coloured pencils are useful for putting down ideas on paper quickly to give an immediate impression of the design. I use soft coloured pencils which also act as watercolour paints. I make a drawing and then use a wet brush to spread the colours or to soften the look of a drawing. I have used these pencils for the coloured drawings in this book. Water-based paints are another useful medium for putting down and recording ideas of a design. A more positive result with brighter colours is possible with the paints than with the pencils.

Scissors are best used for specific jobs. Keep a pair of strong scissors for cutting card and paper only: there is nothing more frustrating than being unable to cut through several layers of paper just at the moment you are ready to do so, and there is nothing that blunts a pair of scissors more than paper.

A knife with a cutting-board and metal ruler makes cutting out straight strips of paper or fabric very quick and easy, but take great care to cut down on to the board (boards are sold especially for this purpose). Keep fingers well out of the way of the knife on a metal ruler: there is a ridged ruler on the market which keeps fingers in a groove away from the edge along which the knife cuts. Rotary or straight-bladed knives may be used for both paper and fabric. I use a general craft knife with easily changeable blades, which is fitted with its own safety blade cover. Knives with sharp blades are less dangerous than blunt ones.

Paper and card are needed for carrying out the design work and for making the pattern pieces of the quilt. Use plain paper for drawing ideas for the quilt; 5 mm (¼ in) squared paper for drawing up the scaled layout of the quilt; thin, cuttable card for making templates; and a variety of coloured and patterned papers for creating designs.

Swiss curves and a flexible curve are useful for drawing curves when you lack confidence in drawing freehand. The flexible curve has the advantage that it can be shaped into the exact curve required for a particular situation.

Sewing tools

Needles are needed for different jobs in the quilt: to apply the pieces to the top of the quilt, to assemble the quilt and to do the quilting. To make the stitches invisible for the appliqué work (or at least as small as possible) a small-eyed 'between' needle, with as small an eye as you can manage, is the best one to use. To make a regular, neat stitch when quilting, use a 'quilting/between' needle. I use a short, small-eyed needle, a 'number 10 quilting/between', for most quilting jobs. If you are new to quilting, however, experiment with various different-sized and different-length needles on a sample of the same type and thickness of fabrics as the quilt to find out which needle you are most comfortable with. Most beginners prefer a firm, long-eyed, long needle but the experienced quilter will use a short, small-eyed and sharp-pointed needle.

Pins are needed to secure the pieces to be applied to the quilt top, and to hold the thickness of the quilt together in its final assembly. It would therefore be useful to have both small, fine pins, and long glass- or plastic-headed pins that will not get lost in the quilt sandwich.

Scissors for appliqué need to be small, pointed and very sharp. I always have a variety of scissors to hand while making a quilt. A pair of snipping cutters are useful for getting close to the surface of the quilt to cut off short thread ends. As I have already mentioned, I keep a separate pair of scissors for paper, as they blunt very quickly and are then not suitable for fabric.

Thimbles are not worn by a large number of sewers today, but they not only help to protect the finger from being constantly stabbed, they help to regulate the hand stitch and give a neat appearance. It takes time to become accustomed to a thimble on the finger, but, with perseverance, you will find that it makes sewing generally more comfortable. There are a variety of thimbles on the market designed especially for specific jobs. The regular thimble should fit the middle finger well: if too small it will feel uncomfortable and if too large it will slip off. In both cases it will just be a nuisance and better not worn. I like the thimble which has a ridge round the head that stops the needle slipping when being pushed hard, and the layered ridges round the side of the thimble are more satisfactory for holding the needle than the conventional indented ones.

Frames are used to hold the quilt layers conveniently stretched while the quilting is in progress. There are numerous different frames on the market: hoop and rectangular, large and small, wooden and plastic.

If you are using the 'quilt-as-you-go' method (see page 26), your quilting pieces will probably be small enough, if well-tacked, to quilt in the hand, but a small hoop may be used. This is like an embroidery hoop, but made of stouter wood to take the weight of the quilt sandwich. This hoop should not be left on the quilt once the day's quilting is finished as it will bruise and crush the fabric of the quilt sandwich. To set it up, place the inner hoop flat on the table and lay the area to be quilted, face up, smoothly over this. Place the outer hoop, with the screws loose, over the quilt on the inner hoop, and then gently turn the screw clamps to tighten the grip on the quilt. The quilt should be stretched on the hoop sufficiently to keep it firm but with enough flexibility for the quilt to move slightly while you are making the quilting stitches.

Large quilting frames are usually too big for the modern house and are very expensive. I have a simple home-made one (see opposite) made from two long and two short battens of wood held together with 'G' clamps to make a rectangle, the ends of which rest on the furniture to allow me to sit at it for quilting. I tack the three layers of the quilt together on a flat surface (usually the carpeted floor) and then sew two opposite ends of the quilt to the webbing which runs along the length of the long battens. I then roll the quilt up around one of these battens, face outwards, until the battens are close enough together to put the short ones in place and secure them with the 'G' clamps. The loose ends of the quilt are kept in place with a tape pinned to the quilt, and are turned around the short battens in the form of a zigzag. The frame is then placed on the furniture ready for quilting.

If you do not have a frame, make sure that you tack the quilt sandwich together thoroughly with lines of quilting 5 cm (2 in) apart in both directions, keeping the quilt completely flat until the tacking is finished. Then quilt it seated at a large table with the quilt folded up and the weight supported by the table, leaving only the immediate area in which the quilting is being done unfolded.

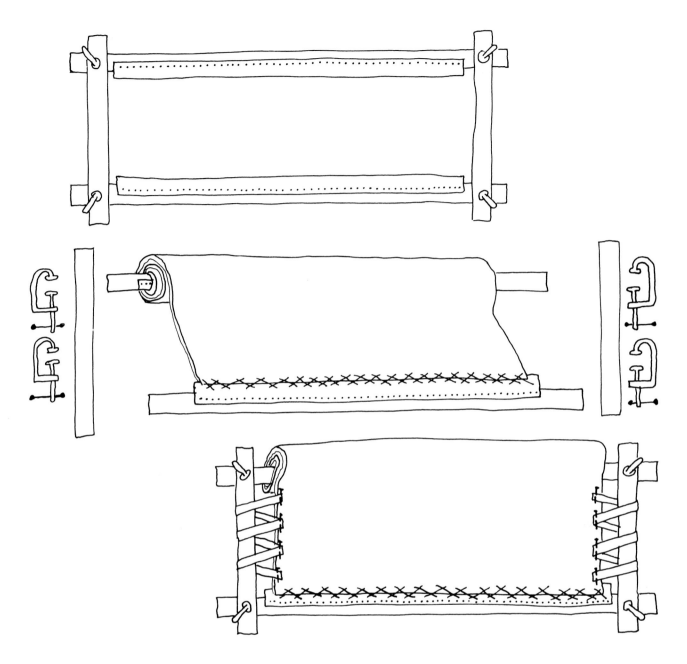

Simple quilt frame showing how to set it up with a quilt

Fabrics

The fabrics you choose will depend on those readily available and those that you like, as well as their suitability for a particular technique. One of the techniques of appliqué, for instance (see page 23) requires a fabric which will turn under easily; a soft lawn responds to being managed in this way whereas a furnishing fabric will not. So how you intend to apply the fabric will determine the types of fabrics for which you will start hunting. Do not be afraid to mix fabrics, because making the whole into a quilt with interlining and backing fabric will even out the weight of the fabrics. Do not be tempted to mix man-made-fibre fabrics with those made of natural fibres, however, as they will not work sympathetically together. Look instead for an alternative fabric in print and colour.

Plain fabrics can help to create a well-defined design, but every stitch used to apply the shapes will show, no matter how skilled a stitcher you are. Limit yourself perhaps to one, two, or three plain fabrics carefully chosen and dispersed evenly over the whole quilt. A textured or glazed plain-coloured fabric will add to the character of the basic plain ones.

The regularity of check fabrics will do well for representing walls of buildings or the weave of a basket, but will show up strongly in contrast to the rounded and soft general characteristics of appliqué.

Striped fabrics, like the checks, are bold and should be placed carefully in the design. Stripes can be used to great effect to create the three-dimensional appearance of a box or a building.

Spotted fabrics can be hard on the eye if used in an unsympathetic way. A minute spot can be used to break the flat effect of plain fabrics and to suggest a slight texture. These fabrics should be used sparingly and with careful consideration. It is not a good idea to select a spotted fabric for a shape when it is only intended to have a support-ing role, as the spots will highlight it.

Geometric prints are often angular in character and will help to set a masculine feel to the quilt, but be careful in using them juxtaposed, as this may cause too much movement in the design and no rest could be sought under such a quilt. The use of plain fabric or soft-coloured natural prints alongside geometric ones could calm down the mood.

Pictorial prints will help to emphasize a part-icular theme in the quilt. A national event is often the source of fabric designs appearing for use in fashion. Flowers and natural-fabric designs are always around in furnishing stores. Make use of them to create a bower of rambling flowers that is both gentle and pretty.

It is worth taking the time to select the right fabrics: I often take up to a year to collect fabrics for a quilt. A new season of prints may supply the appropriate print for a piece of *broderie perse* work (see page 24) to fit in with the theme of the quilt or the weave of a basket.

Supporting materials

Interlinings not only support the whole quilt, but the character of the quilt can change depending on the one that is used. The most commonly used interlining is man-made terylene wadding, as it is readily available in our local shops. It comes in a variety of thicknesses: the thinnest is 50 gm (2 oz); 100 gm (4 oz) is twice as thick; 150 gm (6 oz) is three times as thick, and so on. Many other types of interlining can also be used. An old blanket was used frequently by our ancestors, but in these days of central heating this will make too heavy a quilt. Others possibilities are a flannelette sheet and domette, which will give a thin, flat quilt, and carded wool, silk or cotton wadding which will make a lightweight and soft quilt but one which needs considerably more quilting to keep it stable. Make sure that you know how to deal with any of the interlinings that you choose, and consult the manufacturer if you are in any doubt. Think carefully about the use to which the quilt is to be put and its laundry, as this will help you to decide on the choice of interlining.

Threads need to be strong enough for the job they are going to do. For the appliqué, the sewing will be on the top surface of the quilt and the thread will need to be fine and to match the applied shape in colour (unless a feature is being made of the stitching, in which case the thread will be considered for colour, tone and thick-ness). When using the sewing machine, I would recommend that you use the thread to which you are accustomed and the one which best suits your machine. There is a variety of threads available for quilting, from special quilting threads (both 100 per cent cotton and cotton-covered polyester), to crochet cotton and number 50 sewing thread. I prefer the 100 per cent cotton thread because it is less springy than the poly-ester type. The thickness of the thread will depend on the ease with which it will pass through the fabric that is being quilted. The thread will run through the fabric more easily if you run it through beeswax first. Experiment with various threads on a sample of the quilting sandwich before making a decision.

Embellishments

Different fabrics can create a scene or a special effect in appliqué, but the addition of other materials or objects may produce a clearer image or more pleasing result. Many quilters are not only quiltmakers but also embroiderers, and the two marry together naturally in appliqué work. The use of embroidery can not only be decorative but also the means of recording small details to complete the picture, which in appliqué alone would be impossible. Jean Powell's quilt (see page 93) shows how she has used embroidery to create her own quite individual and unique style. Free embroidery with the sewing machine can resemble drawing on to the surface of the quilt with a pencil, as is illustrated well in the quilt by Joan Fogg on page 20.

There is a great variety of exciting threads manufactured today – metallic, shiny and matt, thick and thin, plied and stranded – which are asking to be used. You could add sparkly interest with buttons, sequins, shells and shisha (mirror) glass, and anything else that takes your fancy.

The Victorians have left us an abundance of ideas in the use of stitchery and applied knick-knacks in their crazy-silk quilts. Ribbons, too, were used abundantly in their quilts; these could be made into roses or some other flower shape and then applied to a quilt. Pieces of lace left over from another sewing job could also be used to add delicacy. So, as well as hunting for fabrics, keep your eyes open for small treasures.

The four seasons *quilt by Rosemary Hesketh, using embroidery to add extra interesting detail. A successful bold design is enhanced by the use of strong colours*

3
Planning the quilt

It is easier to embark on making the quilt if the final situation where the quilt will live is known in the planning stages. If this is the case, the colour and size of the quilt will have been decided, solving the two initial problems.

Measurements

Answer the following questions first:

- Where will the quilt be housed?
- Is it to be for a double or single bed, or a cot?
- If none of these, is the quilt intended to hang on a wall or to cover a piece of furniture?
- What shape will the quilt be? Is it to be rectangular, square or even an unusual shape?

The answers to these questions will have given you the size of the quilt. Make a simple scaled plan of the quilt, recording the size. This can be drawn easily on 5 mm (¼ in) squared paper. You now know exactly the shape and space available in which to start creating the design. I usually make a second copy of the scaled plan, as it easy to destroy the plan when you start to put in design ideas.

Overall design

Record your ideas in the form of thumbnail sketches or words at this stage. If you cannot come up with anything, look further into the book for ideas to start you thinking around the design subject. Within your scaled plan of the quilt, write or sketch the ideas into some sort of arrangement. You could, perhaps, place the main idea in a central square with supporting ideas surrounding it. I seem to use a vast amount of paper at this stage, rejecting and rearranging my ideas until I am satisfied with the final layout (I do not start thinking about details until later). I then colour in the design layout quite generally

with pencils or paint to give me a rough idea as to what the final quilt might look like. One's mind can do fantastic things with a design and these are not always practical; only by making a visual image can one avoid getting as far as having made the top of the quilt before realizing that there is some awful mistake. My advice is therefore to record all ideas and changes while the work is in progress. Look at the drawings of the layout for my *Rondo* quilt (below and opposite) to see this method of working illustrated.

Layout

A bed quilt is a very large object, and at this stage I would experiment with the basic layout, dividing the space up into a set of smaller areas which sit happily together. The design could be like some of the traditional quilts divided into blocks,

*Basic layout of the author's quilt **Rondo** (see page 8)*

16

*Plan of **Rondo***

that is, squares surrounded by individual borders, or a border around a group of squares. The blocks do not need to be set square, but possibly on their points surrounded by triangles to fit into a square or rectangle. Choose shapes which fit into the overall shape: hexagons do not fit well into a square or rectangle, for instance, but diamonds do. Some shapes work well together, such as octagons and squares. The chosen shapes do not have to be the same size, but they do need to

interlock with one another. A large square could be placed within another square, and then within another square, giving a focal point in the centre surrounded by triangles. A border may be added to a shape at any time. Look at the drawings of general layouts overleaf for some examples.

When you have sorted out your ideas, make a drawing of the layout within your scaled plan. From this scaled layout drawing you can multiply up the measurements when the time comes to make templates or patterns.

Suggested layouts for a quilt

Colour

The choice of colour is a very personal one. The situation of the quilt, and for whom it is to be made, will probably govern the basic choice of colour. You may be including realistic concepts in the design which will also influence your decision. The colour of a national flag, for instance, does not change, wherever it is seen. The very nature of appliqué quilts means that a wide range of colours will probably be used. Try to broaden the range to engulf the realistic colours in the overall scheme so that, for instance, the red, white and blue flag sits happily with its neighbouring gentle pink colour scheme. A pink fabric with a red design will help to support the

*These two fabrics were the principal source of the colour scheme for **Rondo** (see page 8)*

red of the flag, but will be barely noticeable within the scheme.

Make a swatch of fabrics in the colour scheme of the quilt required. Do not worry if they are not the actual fabrics at this stage. Include as wide a range of colours as possible, at the same time keeping the character of the quilt. Primary, bright and contrasting colours will create a lively character, while a limited tonal range of colours – whether dark or light – will give a quiet feel.

Colour plan of **Rondo**

Outline of techniques and structure

Record the techniques that you will use and how you plan to assemble the quilt: this can be done on a copy of the scaled layout plan. Doing this will help you to decide on a plan of campaign and to determine in what order the various assignments need tackling. List these assignments and make a rough timetable for each job. Any timetable will probably have to be revised during the making of the quilt. Will the quilt be made using the 'quilt-as-you-go' method (see page 26)? If so, small sections of the quilt will be completed one at a time, limiting the amount of work which has to be done while the quilt is in one whole piece and heavy. Order the techniques to suit your lifestyle.

Quantity of fabric

It is difficult to estimate exactly how much fabric to collect when making such a free design as an appliqué quilt is likely to be. The area of the background, borders and any regular shapes such as one-piece cut-outs can be worked out exactly, along with the backing fabric and the interlining, because you will have made a scaled plan using accurate measurements which will give you the necessary calculation. The quantities for irregular shapes are more difficult to work out, and these could be collected over a long period and in small pieces.

The answer is to start collecting now, even if you are not going to make the quilt until some date in the future. I often take up to a year to collect the fabrics for a quilt, investigating all the possible sources. I will look almost anywhere for unusual fabrics and collect constantly for the quilt in the future. I have ends of lines of fabrics from markets, old clothes made of Indian printed fabrics from jumble sales (washed and given a new life because I like them and one of them might just be the piece for the next quilt), as well as the exotic and simple prints brought back for me from Peru and Malawi. So do not be in a hurry to make a quilt: take time to enjoy collecting the fabrics.

Once you have an idea of the types and colour of the fabrics that you will use in the quilt, make a fabric 'mock-up' of the design. You can do this by cutting out small pieces of fabric and sticking them down on to a copy of the layout plan. Do not spend time being too careful over this, and use pencils and paints to suggest the detail. This will give you a better idea of the finished quilt, and could possibly be made into a card or framed picture to be given with the quilt.

Hot summer *quilt by Joan Fogg showing an interesting use of fabrics coloured by herself*

4
Techniques

Drawing the design

Help with the drawing of the individual design details comes later, in Chapter Five. Do not be embarrassed by a lack of experience in drawing. You are not alone! As I have already said, drawing is only a form of personal note-taking, in the same way that one might jot down words which express an idea. There are many ways of making designs, and drawing with a pencil is only one of them. You will see that I suggest cutting, tearing and folding paper as other ways of obtaining a design.

Reducing and enlarging a design

This is a useful technique to know about. One of the problems with finding a design is that it is often the wrong size for your own needs, and a preliminary sketch may need to be made larger. This is how to translate a design into another size. Draw a regular grid over the original design. Then, on a clean sheet of paper, draw another regular grid which is larger or smaller than the original but with the same number of divisions. Now the design can be drawn into the new grid section by section. The original could be a 5 cm (2 in) grid with a 10 cm (4 in) grid used to make the design larger, or a 2·5 cm (1 in) grid to make the design smaller. It may be possible to achieve exciting new shapes by playing around with the proportions of the basic grid and so altering the outside shape of the design completely.

Template-making

Patterns, or templates as they are known to quiltmakers, are needed to help cut out the shapes required for the appliqué design. Sometimes the templates will need a turning added on to them, and at other times they will need to be the exact size of the shape to be applied.

Templates can be made from various types of material. If only one piece of a particular shape is required, it is sufficient to draw the shape on firm paper, cut it out and use this as the template, but when the template is to be used repeatedly a stronger material will be needed. Sturdier templates can be made from firm card or plastic sheet that will stand up to the constant battering of the pencil tracing round the edge for making numerous cut-out shapes.

How to reduce or enlarge a drawing

Plastic is likely to keep its shape better, but it is not good near an iron. The side of an old ice-cream carton is suitable for templates if it can be easily cut with scissors or a knife. The shape can be drawn on to the plastic with a felt-tip pen, or, in some cases, a soft pencil. Plastic sheets sold especially for the purpose of making templates are available from most patchwork and quilting suppliers.

Card for templates should be firm and easily cut with scissors. This is safe to use in connection with an iron. Cereal packets can be salvaged for templates, the shapes being drawn on the plain side with a pencil and then cut out.

Children's wooden shapes and everyday objects around the home are useful for making easy and quick templates. I have used a child's wooden template of a butterfly in my *Rondo* quilt (see page 8), and a large dinner plate to draw the circle for the 'wreath' block, shown on page 33 (bottom). There is an old quilt in the American Museum in Bath that is full of animals, for which children's shapes could have been utilized. There is probably any size of circle in your kitchen if you look for it.

Cutting out shapes

A soft pencil is ideal for drawing around the templates on the reverse side of the fabric, and a good pair of sharp, pointed scissors for cutting out the fabric shape. If the fabric is dark, a light-coloured or a silver pencil will mark it. You can buy special pens for marking fabric, but I always feel safer with a pencil as I know it is possible to remove the mark with an eraser if I make a mistake, and I am not too sure of the long-term effect of these pens on the fabric. A good pair of scissors will enable you to cut out the minutest of detail, or to cut away completely an unwanted background fabric. Be careful when cutting the background away that you leave enough space around the edge of the shape to accommodate the stitching across the edge or the seam to be turned under when applying.

Placing the shapes

Once you have cut out the shapes, they can be placed on to the base fabric. Appliqué is a very free medium – which is part of its charm – but it can lead to problems of arranging shapes within the space of the quilt: either there is too much

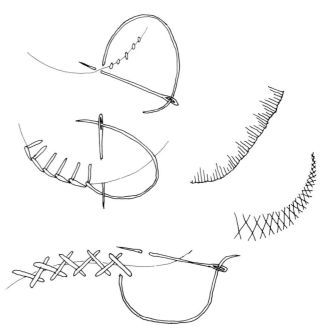

Hemming, buttonhole (or blanket) and herringbone stitches

*Bow from **Rondo** (see page 8), applied with a hemming stitch*

Bow from the border of Pat Salt's quilt (see page 10), applied with herringbone stitch

space left and the applied shapes are floating in mid-air, or the shapes become too crowded.

Whether the base fabric is small or large, it is therefore a good idea to make some guidelines to work on or around. These lines can be folded into or drawn on to the base fabric. The lines can take the form of a grid, or quarter and diagonal lines if the base fabric is a square. If you use a pencil to mark the lines, choose one of a colour that is sympathetic to the quilt. By the time the quilt is finished these lines will have almost disappeared, and what is left will not look dirty or intrusive on the design. If you are not sure about a coloured pencil then do some trials first.

With the lines as a guide, place the fabric shapes down on to the base fabric according to the design, adjusting them until they are in the right position. When they are just right, pin and tack them down about 5 mm (¼ in) inside the edge of the shapes.

Methods of appliqué

Fabric shapes can be applied to a base fabric in a variety of ways, depending on the thickness of the fabric and the effect that is required. Four stitches are commonly used. The simple hemming stitch is barely visible and gives a smooth finish. Buttonhole (or blanket) stitch gives a definite outline to the shape. Herringbone stitch is flexible and follows a complex edge well. A machine zigzag stitch is firm and useful where strength is important, but it can make the fabric feel hard and stiff.

The actual appliqué shape can be cut out exactly and applied directly on to the base fabric without any turnings. In this case the edge would need to be applied with buttonhole, herringbone or zigzag machine stitch in order to cover the raw edge to keep it from fraying. Alternatively, the shape may be cut out with a seam allowance, which is turned under and sewn down with a hemming stitch. The seam allowance can be turned under before applying or as the stitching is being done.

The seam allowance is easily turned under with the help of a card shape cut to the exact size. You could use the cutting-out template for this, providing it is not made of plastic. Place the fabric shape with its added seam allowance face down on the ironing-board and the card shape on top in the centre. Iron the seam allowance over the card. This can then be tacked in place and the

A bird from a printed cotton fabric applied using the **broderie perse** *technique (see overleaf) by Janet Hotten*

shape applied to the base fabric. I clip the seam allowance only when absolutely necessary to ease the turning under. Clipping always leaves a vulnerable area for fraying, and I find that I obtain a smoother line without it. The clips also tend to encourage a jagged edge. Where there is an indent, however, a clip is necessary to obtain a good, clear shape.

Another way to turn the seam allowance over smoothly is to run a gathering thread around within the seam allowance and to pull the thread up around the template before ironing, tacking down and applying to the base fabric. If you run a straight machine line round just inside the seam line, the seam allowance will turn under more easily.

An interlining may be used to make the shape firm and definite. The seam allowance is turned around the interlining, which is cut to the exact shape, tacked in place and applied. Alternatively, an iron-on interlining may be used. The advantage of this is that it can be bought in various weights, and a very lightweight one can be used where the softness of the quilt is important.

Clean, precise shapes may be applied using a bonding agent, readily available from your local

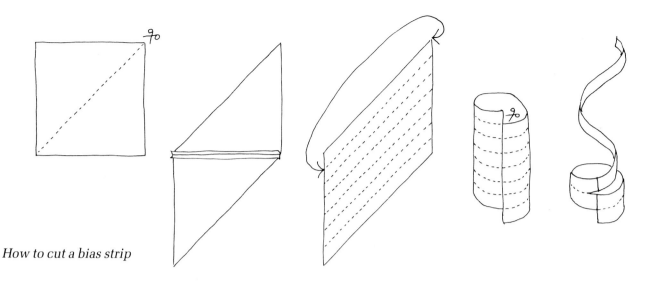

How to cut a bias strip

haberdashery store. Follow the manufacturer's instructions and you should be able to obtain some pleasing results. A bonding agent can be a very useful material, particularly for miniature work, if used with imagination and inventiveness. There are a number of aids like this which claim that you will be able to create perfect appliqué if you use them. Investigate these and experiment to find out whether they are right for you.

When you have applied the shapes, the base fabric behind the shapes may be cut away to give less bulk of fabric in the finished quilt.

Stuffed appliqué

The applied shape may be raised slightly by slitting the base fabric behind the applied shape and stuffing a small amount of teased wadding into the slit before sewing back together. This is a way of giving importance to a focal part of the quilt design.

Broderie perse *appliqué*

This is a style of appliqué used from the eighteenth century onward, in which motifs are cut out from printed fabrics and applied to a base fabric. This could have been done to economize in the use of an expensive material; to use up old favourite pieces of fabric where some of the fabric is worn but other parts still have considerable life left in them; or simply to make use of a particular print of a motif that fits in with the subject of the appliqué. These shapes may be applied using a seam allowance or not as described on page 23. Several of the quilts in this book illustrate the use of this technique.

Shadow appliqué

As its name suggests, this is a way of applying fabrics and then subduing their immediate effect. Brightly coloured fabric shapes are placed on to the base fabric and a see-through layer placed over the top of them. Then a simple running stitch is worked around the shapes, through both the base and the see-through layer, to secure the shapes in place. Organdie or a lightweight cotton lawn could be used for the see-through layer for a less transparent effect. This layer need only cover a group of shapes, not necessarily a complete section of the design. In this case the edge of the see-through fabric must be applied with the appropriate stitch (see pages 22 and 23).

Reverse appliqué

This is when layers of fabric are placed one on top of another and the layers are cut into, the edges of which are turned under and sewn down to reveal the colours of the layers beneath. The Mola work of the Cuna Indians from the San Blas Islands on the coast of Panama and the Pa nDau work of the north Vietnamese people are two different forms of reverse appliqué. The Mola often has a black or red top with many brightly coloured fabrics revealed from beneath to represent exotic creatures. The work is not large and was originally part of the costumes of the Cuna women. The Pa nDau work is made from a single line cut into the top of two fabrics, with either side of the line turned under to make continuous line designs. These designs take the form of grouped spirals or parallel angled lines. Both of these types of reverse appliqué sometimes have the addition of simple embroidery.

Bias-strip appliqué

There are two forms of appliqué using a folded bias strip. One uses the bias strip applied to the base fabric curving round to form a design, and the other uses the bias strip applied over the edges of fabric shapes grouped together and butting up to each other. The first method, sometimes called Celtic work, is useful for applying knot-like shapes, as the bias strip is flexible enough to twist and weave in the way that a knot would do. Pin the bias strip on to the base fabric, with the pins at right-angles to the strip, and follow the design, making the strip weave under and over as appropriate. Tack the strip down and apply using a hemming stitch (see page 22) and hide the end of the strip under a crossing of strips.

The second method is another way of applying grouped shapes without stitching directly across the edges. Place the fabric shapes on the base fabric so that they butt up to each other, tack them down around the very edge of the shapes and apply a bias strip, cutting it to the right length across the join, using a hemming stitch. Continue applying bias strips until all the edges are covered, making sure that the cut ends finish underneath a neighbouring bias strip. When the bias strip used is black, the technique is called stained-glass appliqué.

The strip most commonly used for this work is a 20 mm (¾ in) strip, cut on the bias with the long sides folded into the centre to make it 5 mm (¼ in) wide when folded. The drawing on the opposite page shows how to cut a continuous bias strip.

One-piece appliqué

This is a technique known as Hawaiian appliqué after the beautiful cut-out quilt designs of the late nineteenth century made on the Hawaiian islands. The designs depicted native plants and trees of the islands and were often full-quilt size in red or green on a white background.

Fold up the piece of fabric to be applied and the base fabric into eighths separately and cut a continuous line into the top fabric from fold to fold. Unfold the base fabric and lay it out flat. Place the cut fabric in an eighth on top, and then unfold it, matching fold with fold of the base fabric. Next, tack the cut shape down to the base 5 mm (¼ in) inside the edge and apply it, turning under the edge and hemming. For further information see the drawings under the section on folded cut-outs on pages 62–3. Maggie Davies has used this technique to make her Hawaiian-type quilt *Broken images* (see page 65). She based her design on the acanthus plant in the carving on an old oak banister.

Stitch-and-fray appliqué

This is not yet an established technique, but raw edges are appearing more and more on modern quilts. Stitch down shapes with a machine stitch or a hand stitch without turning or bonding the edge of the shape. The stitching may surround the edge or cross the shape. If a soft edge is required, it is advantageous for the edge to be on the bias, which will let it fluff up rather than losing a wealth of threads by fraying. Experiment with this technique and observe how others are using it.

Assembling the quilt

Joining the top of the quilt

If the top of the quilt has been made up from a series of different-shaped pieces of base fabric, it should be joined together before quilting as a whole piece. Join the pieces together in a logical order, avoiding sewing around an angle if possible. This order should be thought out at the planning stage. It helps to keep the top flat. Blocks can be sewn together in strips and then the strips sewn together. Borders can be sewn on by adding two opposite ones first, followed by the remaining two borders. See the drawing below illustrating the order of sewing *Rondo* together.

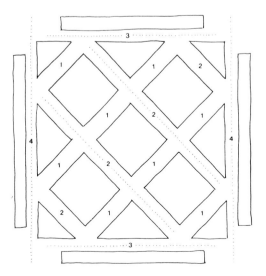

*The order of piecing the top of **Rondo***

25

Quilt-as-you-go

This method of making a quilt is useful for those quilters who do not have much space available for a large quilting frame, or who want to handle the weight of the whole quilt for as short a time as possible. Each section of the quilt is made up and completed, except for the very edge of each section which is left to quilt after all the sections have been joined.

To assemble a section, place the backing piece of fabric face down on the table, the interlining on top and finally the top piece. Pin these three layers together systematically all over, and then tack them first in one direction and then at right angles in rows approximately 5 cm (2 in) apart. Quilt this section, leaving the very edge un-quilted to allow for joining the sections together.

To join two sections together, first pin back the backing and the interlining of the seam to be joined. Pin the tops together face-to-face and seam. Press the seam, being careful not to touch any man-made interlining with the iron. Trim the interlinings so that the edges butt up to one another and ladder-stitch them together. Lay down one of the backing fabrics with the other

one to form a hem, and stitch the hem. Join another section. For a clearer understanding refer to the drawing below, which also shows how *Rondo* could have been assembled using this method. Join all the sections in this way to complete the quilt. Even the borders may be assembled in this way.

Quilt in the whole piece

To assemble the quilt you will need to have the backing fabric and interlining slightly larger than the top of the quilt. Place the backing fabric face down on a large surface (I push the furniture to the walls and use the carpet). Make sure that the back is absolutely flat, keeping it in place with long pins or masking tape if necessary. Place the interlining on to the backing fabric, making sure to keep it flat. Now place the top, face up, on to the interlining, making sure that it is flat and centrally placed. Pin the three layers together in lines approximately 23 cm (9 in) apart. Keep pinning in the same direction so that if the fabric moves it will not wrinkle.

Next, tack the quilt sandwich together in parallel rows going in the same direction, and then in

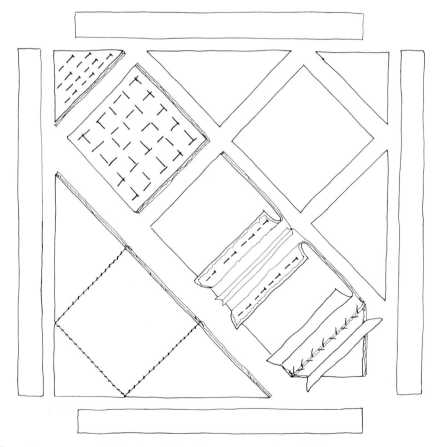

*How **Rondo** could have been assembled using the 'quilt-as-you-go' method*

rows at right angles to the first. These rows should be spaced 7·5 cm (3 in) apart if you will be using a hoop for quilting, and less frequently if you will be using a large rectangular frame. The traditional method is not to tack the sandwich together for a large frame, but I feel that the whole thing is more secure this way. Do what you feel most appropriate for your experience. If the quilt is to be quilted by machine, it is possible to hold the sandwich together by using safety pins. These can be easily removed as the machining progresses and if the layers move irregularly. The quilt is then mounted on a frame (see pages 12–13).

Quilting

Decide on the quilting thread and its colour. A self-toning thread will emphasize the undulating surface created by the stitching; a coloured thread will add to the detail of the quilt story. Take a needle with a thread 25 to 30 cm (10 to 12 in) long and make a single knot in the end. Put the needle into the quilt sandwich and bring it up where the quilting is to begin, pulling the knot into the sandwich. Take one or more stitches on to the needle through the thickness of the sandwich and pull the thread through. Continue in this way until the thread is all used up, then make a knot close to the surface of the quilt, take it through into the middle of the sandwich and trim off the end. Practise the quilting stitch in a similar sandwich to that of the quilt to get the feel of quilting and to achieve as even and as regular a stitch as possible.

The ability to do good machine quilting will depend on your sewing machine and on how experienced a machinist you are. I do use my machine for quilting, but this is usually for the reason that I want to make the article strong and durable, and not for general appearance. Use a long stitch and consider using an invisible thread on the top of the quilt. Be prepared to do something new with the machine quilting, and do not try to imitate the qualities of hand quilting. Experiment!

Knotting

The quilt sandwich may be secured together with a series of knots. This is a method used for joining layers together quickly or for joining a thick quilt sandwich together. The sandwich must be knotted at regular intervals to hold the three layers together securely. The knot consists of a stitch followed by a second stitch on the same spot, the ends of which are tied in a reef knot. Traditionally the ends of the knot are left showing, but many people prefer to hide them back in the interlining.

The edge of the quilt

There is no definitive method for finishing off the edge of the quilt: choose whichever one suits the quilt. You can bind it with either a straight or a bias binding; turn it in and butt it together; lap it to front or back; give it the form of triangles, semi-circles or some other form relating to shapes within the quilt; or insert piping or triangles.

Detail of quilting showing how quilted lines can become part of the design

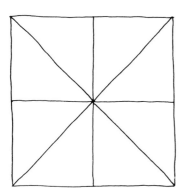

5
The details of the quilt

Layout of small areas

The individual areas of the layout need to be considered for shape, colour and line, and their overall balance with the rest of the quilt. An over-emphasis of one shape, line or colour in an area can upset the complete quilt, so try to make a judgement as to where to place the individual pieces of appliqué within their areas before actually starting to sew. There are several traditional arrangements of appliqué which help to make pleasing results. These take the form either of containers such as baskets, bowls, vases, cornucopia, shells and bows for holding flowers or fruit, or lines on which small shapes may be hung, such as circles to make wreaths, crosses and diagonals of the area, as in the traditional *Rose of Sharon* block illustrated below, hearts for wedding celebrations, spirals, horseshoes, vine trails or ribbons. The quilts shown throughout the book use these ideas.

The lines which divide a layout shape – such as the quarter or diagonal lines of a square, or lines which run from the corners of a triangle to the half division of the opposite side – are ideal lines on which to build an arrangement of applied pieces to use the space well. Alternatively, you can create a freer layout by taking a point within a shape and radiating the lines out from it to the corners and the half points of the sides of the shape, as shown in the drawings on the opposite page (top). Any of the individual shapes may be placed as part of the structure lines. The top of a bowl, for instance, could be placed on the half division of an area so that the lines of the bowl flow into the whole basic design structure.

The basic shape of the container or line may be cut out in fabric and then applied to the base fabric, or the line may be drawn directly on to the base fabric and then flowers, leaves and any other ideas massed on and around the line and applied, giving the appearance of the line.

Shown opposite is a quilt layout which uses the diagonals of the small areas to give a framework on which to place the appliqué. This gives a co-ordinated structure because the lines lead on from one shape to another. Of course one does not have to keep precisely to the framework. A sprig of flowers could be placed off-centre to relieve the monotony of the rigid structure, or an extra bird or butterfly might be placed strategically to stress the focal point of the quilt. Think about this structure carefully, as this is what creates the vital first impressions.

The structure lines of **The rose of Sharon**

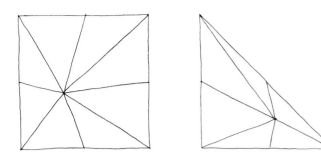

(Left) Lines drawn to an eccentric point to divide up a geometric shape

(Below) Possible quilt layout showing structure lines and how the lines could be used

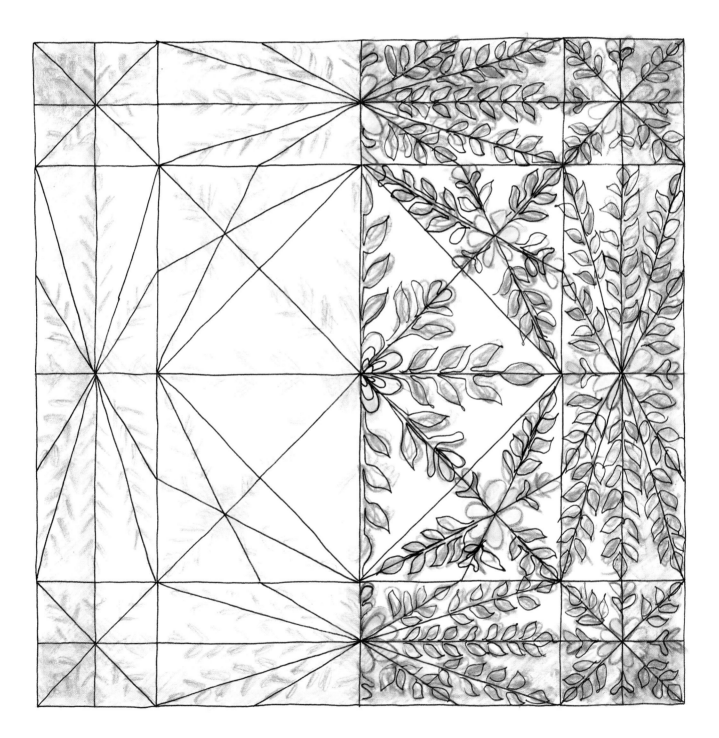

Wreaths

Traditionally, circles have been used to make wreaths of flowers and foliage, as have spirals, crosses, horseshoes and hearts. You can draw circular templates of almost any size with the help of plates and saucers from the kitchen cupboard. Turn a plate upside-down on a large piece of card. Draw round the edge of the plate and cut out the round shape for a template. Old-fashioned meat plates would be useful for drawing large oval shapes. Small circles could be drawn more accurately with a pair of compasses.

Draw three-quarters of a circle to represent a horseshoe. Spirals can be drawn by using a series of circles, graded in size and placed inside each other. Make the outside circle the size of the required spiral. Trace almost round the outside circle, then gently slope the line on to the next circle and draw almost round that circle, slope the line on to the next circle and so on, until you have completed a satisfactory spiral. Adjust the line to make it move gently round and round. Heart shapes, which are also used to create wreaths, are described on page 34. Any of these shapes may be divided into smaller sections: this option has been discussed in the previous section, on page 28.

You can make a wreath from printed flowers and leaves using the *broderie perse* method (see page 24), or design your own flowers and leaves to make a unique garland. Make a template for the basic shape of the wreath, and use it to draw the line of the wreath directly on to the base fabric. Then build up the flowers and foliage to be applied on to the line to complete the wreath. Alternatively, cut a bias strip of fabric (as shown on page 24) and tack and apply it to the base fabric, following the line of the wreath, before applying the shapes around the bias line.

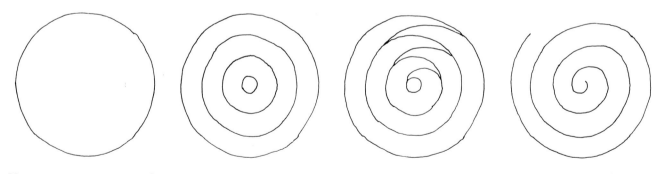

How to construct a spiral

Wreaths in the traditional colours of green and red in the shapes of hearts, circles, spirals and a cross

*A graceful arrangement of a wreath of tulips by
Rosemary Hesketh*

(Above) A generous wreath of pink roses by Pat Salt

(Left) A wreath of delicate flowers and leaves linked by lines of quilting

Hearts

Hearts can be drawn easily by grouping three circles together and using their combined exterior shape as a guide for the drawing. Draw three circles grouped together as if they were to fit in a triangle. Then take the shape of two of the circles to make the top of the heart, add a point or a small triangle on to the other and join this circle up to the other circles with straight or slightly curved lines as shown below. You now have a heart shape. To vary the character of the heart, group the three circles differently before making the outline.

You can use the heart as a frame on which to place a wreath, or group hearts to make pleasing designs. Pile different-sized hearts on top of each other or butt them up to each other to produce interesting negative shapes (negative shapes are those created between the main shapes). Lines cut into the inside of the heart can create ideas for reverse appliqué (see page 24). Look at the coloured drawing opposite for ideas.

Make the necessary templates, adding seam allowances if necessary. Cut out the fabric and apply in the appropriate way.

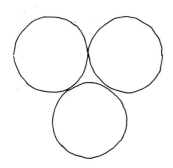

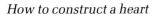

How to construct a heart

34

Heart shapes stacked together and used to create a border

Bowls and vases

The shapes of bowls and vases can be drawn by basing them on circles, for which templates of any size can be drawn using a pair of compasses. Draw a circle of the correct size for the main body of the vase. Then draw two small circles, touching but not overlapping the first circle, symmetrically on either side near the top of the circle, and join these with a straight line that touches the top of the two small circles. Now draw two more small circles touching and near the base, so that they are symmetrical on either side of the circle but closer together than the top two, and join them with a straight line that touches the base of the small circles. Select the outline of the vase from this drawing. The shape and character of the vase can be varied by changing the proportion of the circles to one another. Experiment with different sizes of circles, and with the position of the horizontal lines, until you have a pleasing outline. The shape of the vase is more important than absolute accuracy in the drawing, unlike the blocks drawn for piecing.

To design a bowl, draw two circles of the same size, touching and on the same level. Draw smaller circles in the same way as for the vase,

but this time at either side of the two circles at the top and base, again joining them with straight lines to obtain the top and the base of the bowl.

You can draw elegant curving handles for the bowls or vases by using larger secondary circles at the top, perhaps combining two or more circles for more complex or ornate handles. The right size of circle might make your vase into a jug. Look at the coloured drawing opposite for ideas. The spiral handles illustrated are made by drawing a spiral into the circle which forms the handle. To make these in the fabric, simply cut a single spiral line into the circle of fabric where the handle is. Tack down the fabric and then apply the fabric by sewing down both sides of the cut spiral line, turning under the edge as you go. This makes very decorative spirals, such as those in the Pa nDau work of the Hmong people of north Vietnam.

If you do not like the curved lips of your bowls and vases, use straight vertical lines instead of curves at the relevant points. Experiment to obtain new bowls and vases. Make the templates, adding seam allowances if necessary, cut out the fabric and apply as appropriate.

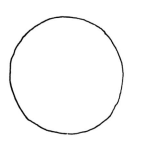

How to draw a vase

How to draw a bowl

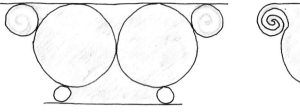

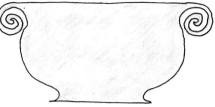

Bowls, vases and jugs suitable for fruit or flowers

(Left) A lavishly filled bowl with a reverse-appliqué handle by Pat Salt

(Below) A classical bowl of flowers in a conventional arrangement

A blue pottery vase of flowers by Jean Powell makes a pleasing block

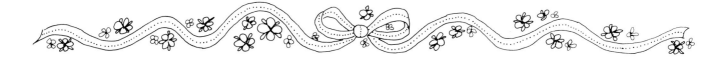

Bows

To draw a bow, first tie a bow in ribbon or cord. Spread it out flat on a clean piece of paper and draw round the edge of it. You will probably want to round off or clean up the edges to make it look more realistic. Another method is to make up a bow from its basic shapes, which are simply three circles and two straight shapes or any variation of these formal shapes. The straight shapes can be tapered with a 'V' snipped into one end.

There are a number of printed fabrics patterned with bows in fabric shops. You can cut these out and use them in the *broderie perse* method (see page 24), cutting them in such a way as to make the ribbon go just where you want it by discreetly turning its direction under a flower or a leaf. Actual ribbon bows could also be applied to the base fabric. One bow shape on top of another gives a feeling of generosity and abundance: you could have a slightly smaller and light-toned bow placed at a slight angle on top of a larger and darker one. The ends could be left free to float or sewn down. Adding seam allowances if necessary, make templates for the complete bow or for the individual shapes which make up the bow, as illustrated in these drawings. Cut out the fabric and apply as appropriate.

A suggestion of how to assemble a bow with several variations

*A bow around a bunch of flowers and bows with long
flowing ribbons as borders*

(Left) Holly wreath tied with a flouncy red bow by Rosemary Hesketh

(Below) A bouquet of roses held with a bow created from printed ribbons by Pat Salt

Sprays of flowers with a navy bow

Shells

Clamshells can also be drawn with the help of a circle. Draw a circle the size of the required shell and divide the circumference into an even number of sections with the help of a protractor. Draw a bumpy line round the circumference of the circle with the help of a coin or other round object that fits neatly into a section. Make one of these bumps at the base of the circle into a complete circle, and mark a point on the circumference of this circle towards the centre of the large circle. Join this point up with the bumps, using slightly curved lines to give the ribs of the shell.

You can draw shells into an oval in a similar way, giving a more elongated look. Try experimenting, too, with other shell shapes. Use a basic triangle or square shape, with the edge divided up and rounded into small, curved bumps, and add the ribs across the shape to make a shell.

Make the templates, adding seam allowances if necessary. Look for fabrics which suggest the texture of the shell, or embroider the texture and ribs on to the applied shape. The template may also be cut in sections of the shell, which will allow you to make each section a different colour or graded in tones of one colour.

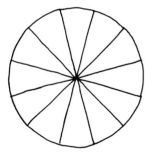
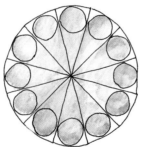

How to construct a shell

Luscious shell shapes based on circles, ovals and triangles

Cornucopia

To draw a cornucopia first draw a circle with a circumference of the same outer curve as the required horn. Draw in the diameter of the circle and, on this, draw another circle smaller than the first, which touches the circumference of the circle and has its centre on the diameter. This drawing will give you the outline shape of the horn. To vary the fatness of the horn, change the size of the small circle: up in size to obtain a slender horn and down in size to create a plump one.

To give the horn ribs along its length, draw more circles at regular intervals, with their centres on the diameter of the first circle and also touching the circumference in the same place, as shown. To draw ribs going across the horn, draw in angles at the centre of the small circle. You can make the edge of the horn bump regularly and realistically within these angles, perhaps using a coin or series of coins. Lips to the horn, and a curly end, can be created using circles in a similar way to those on the bowls and vases on pages 36–7, as shown in the drawing below.

Make the templates from the drawings, adding seam allowances if necessary. Look for fabrics which suggest the texture of the cornucopia, or embroider the texture and ribs on to the applied shape.

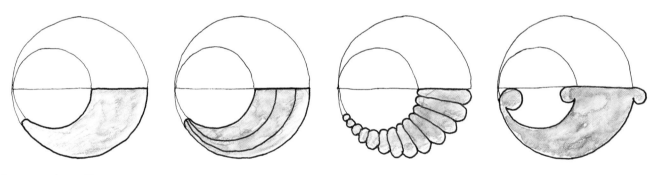

A suggestion of how to construct cornucopia

*Four overflowing horns of plenty surrounded by a
swag border*

Cornucopia full of flowers by Jean Powell

(Opposite) Another cornucopia overflowing with flowers

Baskets

You can choose from many shapes of baskets for filling with fruit or flowers. The simplest can be created from a square. Draw a square roughly the size of the basket you require and round off the corners. Draw a dividing line horizontally across the middle. In the top half, draw a line parallel with the outside and the width of the handle away from the outside. You now have a basket shape. A round basket can be drawn in a similar way. Start with a circle and draw in the diameter, then draw a line inside at a handle distance and parallel with the circumference in the upper half. The base of the basket will need flattening slightly. Similarly, a gondola-type basket can be drawn by first drawing a circle and then an oval inside the circle near the top.

You can make up the basket from one shape, or from fabric strips woven together to give the texture of a cane weave. Assemble the handles from plaited or twisted strips of fabric, or use bias or straight-folded strips, depending on whether the pieces need to describe a curve. Several of the quilts in this book have baskets in them – find the one which appeals to you. Perhaps you have a fabric whose print looks just like a basket weave. Make suitable templates, adding seam allowances if necessary, cut out the fabric and apply in the appropriate way.

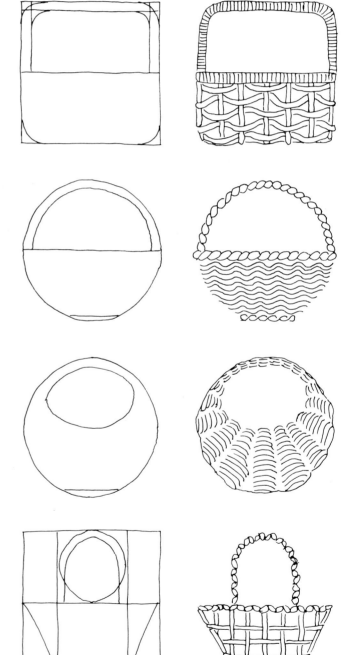

How to draw four simple baskets

*Five different country baskets, including a traditional
pieced one suitable for filling with fruit and flowers*

(Above) A basket of flowers, showing the use of a printed fabric to suggest a basket weave, by Janet Hotten

(Left) A profusion of flowers in a basket by Jean Powell

A delightful basket of summer flowers by Rosemary Hesketh

A country basket with roses by Pat Salt

An elegant basket of flowers

Trails

Trails are useful for filling borders or empty spaces. A line can be drawn across a space or along a border area and then adorned with leaves, fruit, flowers, twigs or twirls. To draw a curving vine-trail line you could make a curve with a piece of string placed flat on a sheet of paper and draw along its length, or you could shape a flexible curve to the required gentle, flowing line and use this as a template, drawing along it and moving it along until the line is the required length. This will help you to make just the right curve and even to take a trail round a corner satisfactorily, as you can keep on changing the shape of the string or flexible curve to suit any situation. Trailing ribbons can be drawn in the same way, possibly drawing along both sides of the curve to make the width of the ribbon. Experiment with the flow of the line, making it angular or smooth and gently curving according to the character required.

Make templates by drawing and cutting out the required curve along one side of a rectangle of card, adding seam allowances if necessary. Bias strips of fabric can be applied in a soft curve to give the character of rampaging vines. Apply leaves or any other shapes along the trail to complete the picture.

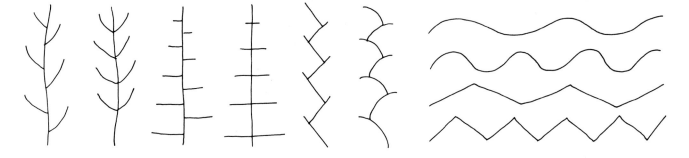

Structure lines for trails and sprays

*Frames within frames, showing a flowing vine trail,
a trail based on a zigzag and sprays, with a medallion
wreath*

Trees

Trees have long been the foundation for designs on textiles. They are useful because they will cover what is otherwise a large and empty space. They can fill a large central area, important in its own right, or be used to fill an awkward corner. Having decided on the area to be covered by the tree, you can simply cut a trunk straight out of fabric, place it centrally and then randomly cut out branches and twigs, applying them as you go. This will give you a feeling of freedom to accommodate any shape of space available and to make enough room for special pieces that you wish to hang on the tree, such as a beautiful bird or an exotic fruit.

To obtain a symmetrical tree, fold a piece of paper the same shape and size as the space available in half vertically and cut out the shape of half a tree, remembering that the trunk will lie along the fold. If you feel confident, you could then cut directly into the fabric by folding the piece of fabric in half and cutting out half the tree, just as with the paper. Otherwise, work until you have a satisfactory tree, and I would suggest that you try several before you make any decisions. Use the paper cut-out as a template for the actual cut-out in fabric. Take half of the paper tree and pin it to the folded fabric, again remembering where the trunk of the tree is, and cut out round the template, not forgetting to add a seam allowance if required. A folded line or a pencil line on the base fabric will help you to place the tree down on to it in the correct position. This is the method used to place down one-piece cut-outs as seen on the Hawaiian quilts and described on page 25.

Experiment with the different shapes of trees. Try those with leaves on, or those with groups of leaves clustered together, making one shape on the end of a branch. Look at books on trees which

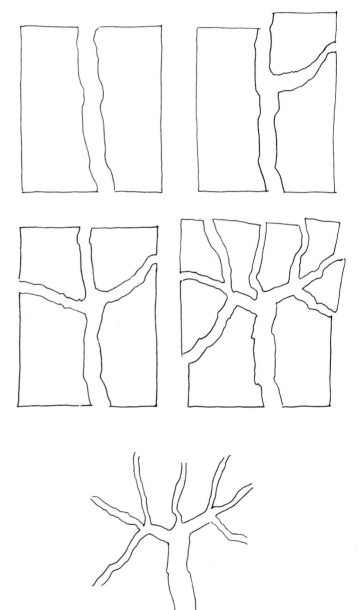

Cutting or tearing a paper rectangle to make a tree

A season of trees

A simple tree by Jean Powell

show the tree not only in full leaf but also in its winter form, revealing the outline shape and the formation of its branches. There are enough ideas there to make a quilt on the subject of trees alone.

Another way to design a tree is to play around with cutting into or tearing a single rectangle of paper (see the illustration on page 56). It is easier to see what you are doing if you work with two papers which contrast with one another, such as black on white. Take a rectangle of black paper considerably smaller than the tree you require, and a large sheet of white paper, possibly of the shape and size for which you are designing. Cut freely into the black paper. Cut or tear the paper in half vertically, not necessarily with a perfectly straight line. Lay the two pieces of paper down on the white one, arranged slightly apart and adjusted to look like the trunk of a tree. Pick up one half, and this time cut through it at an upward angle before placing it down on the white paper again, in its right place but slightly apart.

The tree now has a trunk and one branch. Go on cutting into any of the pieces of paper and pulling apart as you place them down until you have a satisfactory tree. Stick the black pieces down on to the white to record the design. To make a template, trace the design on to paper and either use this as the template to pin on to the fabric for cutting out, or transfer it to something thick to make a more permanent template. Remember to add a seam allowance if necessary. Cut out the fabric and apply in the appropriate way.

Folded cut-out tree with falling autumn leaves by Rosemary Hesketh

Leaves

The easiest way to draw leaves is to pick some and draw round their edges. If these drawings are too large or too small, they can be brought into the correct scale by reducing or enlarging them on a photocopier or by the method described earlier on page 21. Leaves are often grouped in nature, so take time to look at some of the things you are trying to portray and analyse their appearance. Are the leaves pointed or round? Are they arranged alternately or opposite one another on the stem? If the leaves appear to be in groups, are they in fact one large leaf or made up of a number of different ones? Do these vary in size? Are the stems stiff and straight, or do they curve? Look too at the angle of the leaves on a stem. All these observations will help you to make decisions about those on the quilt. If it is the wrong time of year then there will be plenty of reference books on the subject in your local library.

Cut out some paper leaves and a stem and try making different arrangements with them so that you know about the layouts when you are ready to use the leaves with flowers or fruit. Do not always be symmetrical in your arrangements. Try making arrangements of an odd number of objects, and try cutting leaf shapes out freely without drawing them first: think of the scissors as a tool that will make a line like a pencil. If you can master this fear of always having to draw something first you will have acquired that freedom which will enable you to make a relaxed design in the future.

Make templates from the drawings, adding seam allowances if necessary, cut out the fabric and apply the leaves as desired.

Leaf shapes traced from actual leaves

Leaf shapes taken directly from the garden

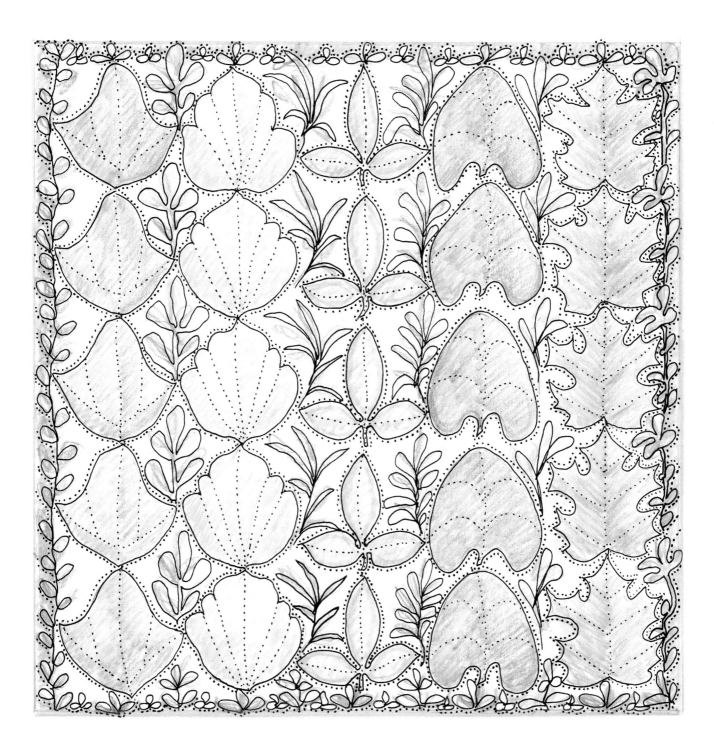

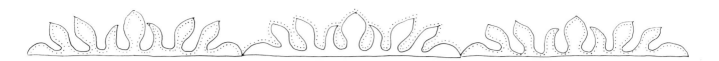

Folded cut-outs

This traditional method, used by the Hawaiians, is a good basic way of designing to fill an expansive area. Different shapes such as flowers and butterflies can be added, and it makes in itself interesting and highly decorative patterns. This method of appliqué is described earlier in the book on page 25. Take a piece of thin paper slightly larger than the required design and fold it in the same way as described for the fabric. Draw on to the top section of the paper a continuous line from one folded edge to the other. This is the cutting line. You can make this line as complicated as you wish, but you should still think of it as a continuous line. In this way you will design an interesting outline for the cut-out. Base the line on shapes such as flowers, leaves or fruit, which are the traditional subjects used by the Hawaiians. You could draw half a flower shape along one fold and another on the other fold, and join them up with a group of leaves or even the outline of a butterfly or bird.

The basic shape with which you start does not have to be a square. I have a border round my *Rondo* quilt cut in this way from large triangles, using flowing leaves as a basis for the design (see page 8). Try using some of the shapes and methods for drawing shown under the other subjects in this chapter.

When you have decided on the design, cut along the folds of an eighth of the cut-out, adding a seam allowance if necessary. This will give you the template to use on the fabric. If you are going to use it more than once you will need to make a stronger template first. Cut out the fabric and apply as described on page 25.

How to fold and cut paper or fabric for a one-piece design

62

*A folded cut-out design showing the contrasting effect
of using different fabrics*

Folded cut-out centre surrounded by quilted flowers and a frame made from a trail of flowers. Note how Monica Dunning has used the same flower shape in different contexts to great effect

***Broken images** quilt by Maggie Davies using the Hawaiian one-piece cut-out technique (see page 25) in a bold colour choice. The rhythmic cut was made from a fold in four, not eight, to accommodate the rectangular shape of the quilt*

Suns

The circle is a good basic shape to use for designing, as we have seen with some of the other subjects. Alterations to the edge of the circle will make it into a sun, a star or a mariner's compass, which are just a few of the traditional appliqué designs.

To design a sun, draw a circle the size of the required design, and another, smaller circle with the same centre inside the first. Divide the circle up into sixteen regular sections using a protractor. Join the points alternately from the outer circle to the inner circle all round the edge. You will have made a circle with a zigzag edge which could be a sun. This edge can be varied by dividing the circle into more sections and by making the two circles closer together or further apart. The type of edge may be varied by using a curved instead of a zigzag line. You could do this by finding a round shape such as a coin that fits into the section and then drawing round it, or by taking a pair of compasses with the radius equal to a section of the circle and drawing a semi-circle at alternate points on the inner circle. A further variation can be made to the basic sun by cutting shapes into the body of the sun.

Make a template for the whole of the shape, keeping it as round as possible and adding a seam allowance if necessary. Fabric moves out of shape easily sometimes, and a more satisfactory result may be achieved by using a large, round template rather than one which represents only a section of a circle. Cut out the fabric and apply the shape to the base fabric using the appropriate method.

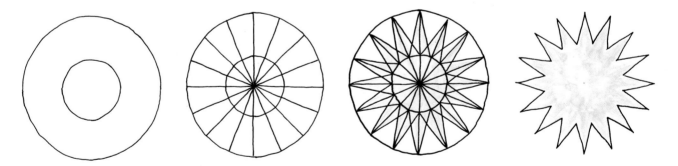

How to draw a sun

66

A sun showing a variety of rays of different proportions

Stars

A simple eight-pointed star can be drawn on a four-by-four grid. Draw a square the size of the required star and divide it up with a four-by-four grid. Then, following the drawings shown here, draw in the diagonals of some of the small grid squares to give you the outline of the star (this is not a true eight-pointed star). Remove any unwanted lines. You can vary the character of the star by altering the grid, as shown.

To obtain a true star you need to draw a circle the size of the required star and another circle with the same centre but half the radius of the first one. Divide the circle into sixteen by drawing in the diameter and then dividing up the centre, using a protractor to mark off angles of 22·5°. Then join these divisions alternately on the two circles. You now have a regular eight-pointed star.

You can make a six-pointed star by first drawing a circle the size of the required star. With the same radius, mark off six points round the circumference. Join alternate points to obtain the outline of the star.

To make the points of either star longer, draw in the lines joining opposite points. Mark off a point at a regular distance outside the star on each of these lines, and join them up with the inner points of the star. Any point along these lines may be taken to elongate or reduce the length of the points.

Make a template of the star, adding a seam allowance if necessary. To make the points as neat as possible, turn and tack under the turning before applying. This will not make sharp and pristine points, however, because there is too much fabric to turn under in a limited space, and the turning at the inner points of the star will need snipping. It is also possible to make up the star using the traditional English patchwork method of piecing diamonds over papers, joining them into a star shape and then applying. You can create decorative designs by cutting lines into the body of the star fabric and sewing down either side of these lines to the base fabric to produce delicate patterns like the Pa nDau patterns of the Hmong people from north Vietnam.

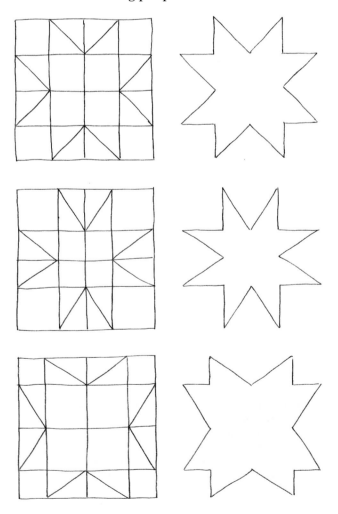

How to draw star shapes using a four-by-four grid

Stars of different shapes in a pale blue sky

Flowers

There are hundreds of flower shapes from which to take your designs. Here are some simple ways of producing just a few of them using straight-forward paper cuts. Take a square of thin paper, such as greaseproof or layout paper, the size of the required flower. Fold it in half, then into quarters and then into eighths. Make sure that you know where the centre of the piece of paper is. Draw a petal in this eighth, as shown in the drawing below, and cut through all the layers around the outside of this shape from diagonal fold to the other diagonal fold. Unfold to reveal the flower shape. Vary the shape of the petal to make a different character of flower. With this fold you will always obtain a flower with eight petals or a multiple of eight. Try folding the paper into a different number of sections, or fold an angle of 60° to give a six-petalled flower, but always remember where the centre of the paper is or you will have petals floating everywhere.

A flower can be made up of individual petals, and these could vary slightly in shape and sit round a central axis to make a more realistic-looking flower. As with leaves, the individual petals of a real flower could be placed flat on a sheet of paper and traced round. A template can then be made from this drawing. Remember to add a seam allowance if necessary.

Flowers do not have to be symmetrical, so make some petal-shaped templates, draw round them and group the petals into the shape of a snapdragon or a pansy. Give different centres to a flower by placing one shape on top of another in the appliqué process. A five-petalled flower can have a spiky centre, such as a *hypericum*, or a *convolvulus* may have a dark centre. Use the petal templates to make a further multiple-petalled template, or use the template to cut out petals to be applied one by one.

An alternative way to design flowers is to use a series of curved patches. Make a group of small squares with a quarter-circle drawn on to some of them. Play around with these, putting them into different arrangements, and you will come up with some flower shapes such as the one illustrated on the opposite page (top). When you have a pleasing shape, stick the squares down on to paper, trace off the flower shape and make a template to use with the fabric.

If you are familiar with the English patchwork method of piecing diamonds together over papers, you can form angular flower shapes such as the American peonies or cactus rose of the early nineteenth century. The 60° or the 45° diamond can be used for this. Some will look like flowers and others like buds, depending on

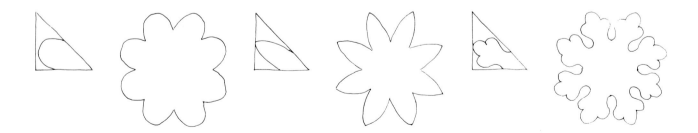

How to create flowers with a folding-and-cutting approach

whether you use, one, two, three, four or more diamonds. Use these in conjunction with free-flowing stems to make them feel more natural. Assemble the diamonds over papers in the traditional way, remove the papers and apply the flower shape to the base fabric. Experiment with the various methods of designing flowers and make an attractive arrangement.

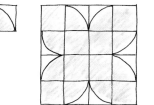
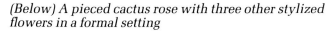

(Below) A pieced cactus rose with three other stylized flowers in a formal setting

(Above)
How to create flowers using geometric shapes

(Left) A group of flowers with a charming butterfly by Jean Powell

(Opposite) Detail of exquisite machine embroidery on applied flowers by Joan Fogg

(Below) Flowers with added embroidery detail by Rosemary Hesketh

Fruits and berries

Apples are round, so the circle comes in use again to draw these. Draw a circle the size of the required apple. Make a small, not quite symmetrical dent in the top and the bottom of the circle. Draw a short curved line in the top dent to represent the stalk and a little scribble in the bottom dent to act as the dried flowerhead, and there you have an apple.

Pears can be drawn in a triangle. Draw a triangle roughly the size of a pear, and in it draw a circle to touch all three sides of the triangle. Take one of the corners of the triangle and round it off. You now have the shape of a pear. Make a slight dent in the apex and add a stalk, and at the base of the pear make another dent for the dried flowerhead, as with the apple.

Bananas can be drawn using a quarter-circle. Draw a quarter-circle with another quarter-circle inside and parallel with it. Round both ends of the quarter-circles, making one slightly angular and squarish, and add a short, stumpy stalk at the other. Another curved line from end to end of the banana will make it more realistic.

Bunches of grapes can be drawn in a triangle. Draw a triangle large enough for masses of little circles to be drawn inside it. Draw small circles completely filling the triangle, with a few overlapping the edge. Add a curved line to one side of the triangle. Adjust as necessary, and this should now look like a bunch of grapes. The design can be applied as one shape, or the individual grapes can be applied one at a time to build up the bunch, remembering the triangle as the basic shape. Individual grapes can also be made as Suffolk puffs and turned over before applying. Berries and cherries can be made individually

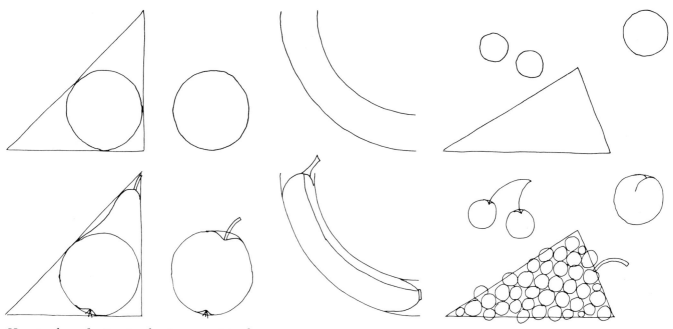

How to draw fruit using basic geometric shapes

74

like this too, to give them a little natural plumpness. Make the templates for the individual pieces of fruit, adding seam allowances if necessary, and make an arrangement of fruit in a bowl or a basket. The colour chosen for the fruits, along with the embroidered or even painted details, will also add to the realism. Cut out the fabric and apply in the appropriate way.

A harvest of fruit

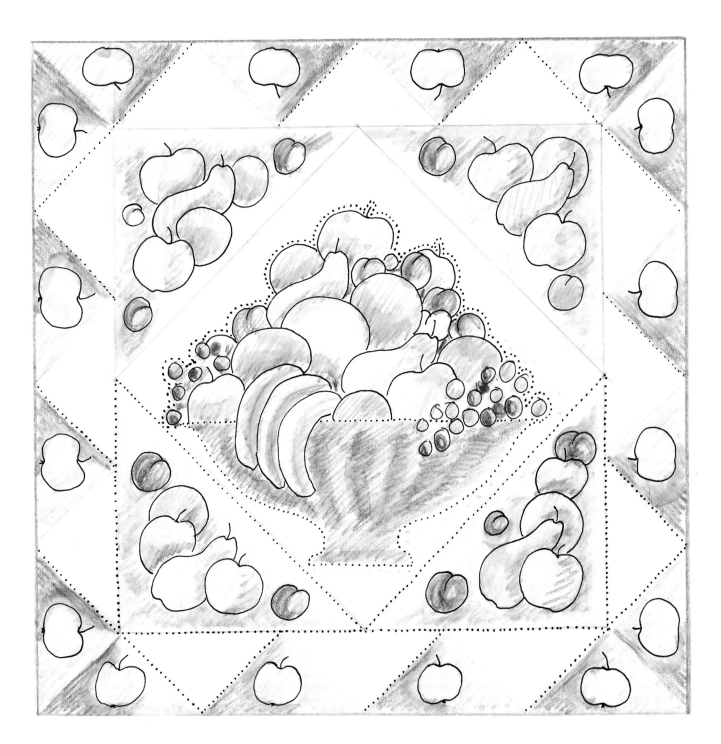

*Bowl of fruit by Joan Fogg. Some detail has been
imaginatively added with a paintbrush*

*Details from **The four seasons** by Rosemary Hesketh showing tulips, holly leaves with berries, fruit with a ladybird, and a butterfly*

People

If you have not had much drawing experience, it is natural to think it impossible to draw such complicated things as people. But one only has to think about cartoons, and about how one reads the image and recognizes people with the merest suggestion of a line or characteristic, to realize that the image of a figure can be quite simple. Do not try to be clever and expect your drawing to have every detail in it. When drawing people the proportion of the body is important, and the detail of a skirt on one short figure and trousers on another will tell someone that this is a picture of a girl and a boy. There is no need to portray details of hairstyle or facial features. So, when thinking of designing people for a quilt, keep them simple: complicated details will only emphasize the ill-proportioned figure and one's lack of knowledge.

You can group figures in lines or in circles using the paper-cut-out method of designing. Think about how many head measurements will make the height of a figure (seven for adults and five for children, although of course this can vary) and how long the legs and arms are compared with the body. Be critical about your proportions, altering them as necessary, and things will appear quite normal.

Now make a cut-out. Take a length of thin paper and fold in half again and again until you have the proportion that you think will do for a person, ensuring that there is not too much paper in the folds to cut through. Against one of the folds, draw a line to represent half a person with their arm stretching across to the other fold (see below). Alter your drawing as necessary, and then cut out along the drawing line. Unfold the paper and you should have a line of people. They will probably resemble the figures of an eastern European peasant embroidery.

Try the same thing again, but this time use a circle of paper which is folded in half, quarters, eighths and sixteenths, and draw the half figure along either of the folds with the head into the middle or to the outside. The next variation is to try to cut a boy down one fold and a girl down the other holding hands. Cut and cut until you have something you think you can apply. The less complicated the outline, the easier it will be to sew. A section of the paper cut-out may be used as a template for cutting out the fabric. Fold the fabric as you did the paper, pin the template on to the folded fabric and, with sharp scissors, cut out the fabric, using the template as a guide and remembering to add a seam allowance if

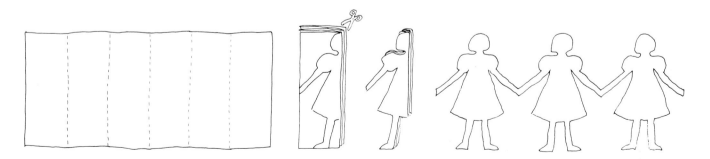

A line of girls cut from folded paper

required. Open out, tack down to the base fabric and sew in place.

The people may be used individually if required, and features could be added to the applied figure as appropriate in the form of pieces of fabric or embroidery. Once again, keep it simple.

'Ring a ring o' roses'

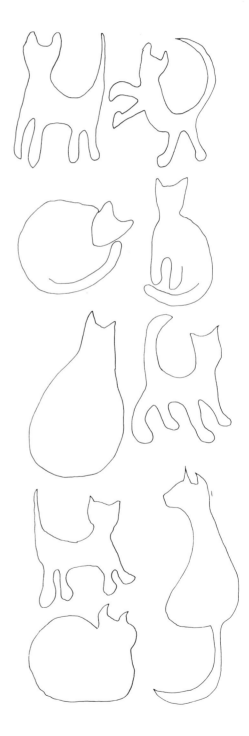

Animals

Animals are fairly difficult to draw, so a child-like approach would perhaps be the most straightforward way to start out. Think about the animal and its basic shape: for example, a cat has a head with pronounced ears and eyes, four legs, a squarish body and a long tail. Start to draw the outline of the cat with his ears, and, without taking your pencil off the paper at all, continue drawing the entire cat in this way, not forgetting to put in all the features you thought of at first. Continue drawing several cats in this way until you have achieved a pleasing outline.

A similar method is to draw the animals using squared paper as a guide. Thinking of the features of the animal, draw its outline, following the lines and diagonals of the squares. When you have finished, you will probably need to round off the shape of the animal.

You may need to enlarge your final drawing. Do this by the method described on page 21 or with a photocopier until the animal is the right size. Make a template, adding a seam allowance if necessary, cut out the fabric and apply as appropriate.

Experiment by drawing a farmyard or a zoo of animals in this way, emphasizing the different characteristics of the animals.

Simple one-line cat shapes

80

Family of cats used to make an amusing panel

Butterflies

Butterflies add a point of interest to a bouquet or a vase of flowers, and provide the opportunity to use different types of shapes together. They can be drawn using four circles grouped together as a guide, or by taking a rectangle of squares and following the lines and diagonals of these squares to describe the four sections of a butterfly's wings. Details of the body and the antennae may be added with embroidery at the appliqué stage. See the drawings below for ideas.

You can make templates either for the complete butterfly or for the individual parts of the wings. If you choose the latter, the wings can be arranged at a slight angle to make it appear that the butterfly is flying. Remember to add a seam allowance if necessary. You might like to select parts of patterned fabrics specially to create exotic species. Cut out the fabric, apply as appropriate and add details if desired.

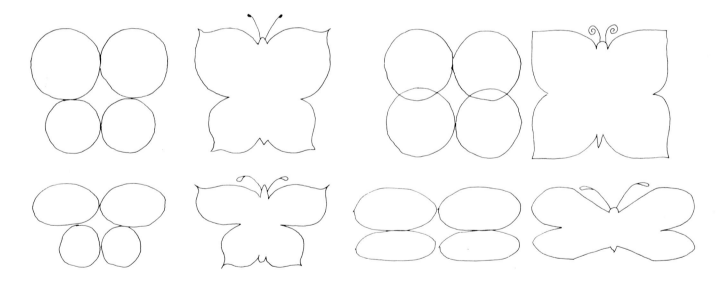

Butterfly drawings based on circles and ovals

*Fritillary of butterflies in an ordered arrangement
showing interesting negative shapes*

Knots

There is a wealth of knots in various forms of art from which we can take ideas. The lover's knot in our own tradition of quiltmaking is the obvious one with which to start. Once you have drawn one knot, you will have some idea of how to copy others that you find.

To draw the lover's knot, start with a square divided by the quarter lines and plenty of space all round. With a pair of compasses, and with a radius of half the length of the square and the point of the compass on the corner, draw a quarter-circle within the square. Repeat this at each corner. Then, with the compass point on the centre point of each side and the same radius, draw semi-circles within the square. Now, with a radius of a quarter the length of the side of the square and the point of the compasses on the outside quarter points of the sides, draw eight semi-circles. To make a double line, repeat the drawing from the same points but make the radius 5 mm (¼ in) smaller each time. Take each crossing of lines and rub out two lines to make one appear to cross the other. Make this happen alternately by tracing round the knot. Take away all the straight lines and you have a lover's knot. The character of this knot may be changed by varying the proportion of the arcs that are drawn.

Try to design your own knots using squared paper and a pair of compasses. The art lies in getting the lines to interweave with one another. If you have drawn them regularly, every time a line crosses another make them pass alternately under and over. Some other knots are shown in the coloured drawing opposite; try to draw them to size and to fit your own shape.

Make a template for the knot: this need only be a quarter of the knot, as the shape is repeated in each quarter. Tack down and apply a bias strip (as described on page 25) on the lines of the knot.

Experiment with the colouring of the bias strips. You could perhaps interweave one colour with another for an interesting effect.

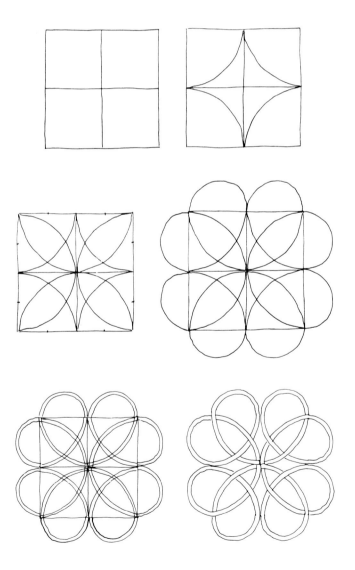

How to draw the lover's knot

A sampler of knots

Birds and fish

Simple curved and flowing lines can be used to suggest birds and fish. Practise just drawing lines with a soft pencil on plain paper: lines with gentle curves, small curves, deep curves and a mixture of all three.

Now try drawing these curves in conjunction with one another, making the curves go in the same direction but not necessarily always at the same distance away from each other. See if you can get them to look like a bird, adding an eye and tail as required. It is possible to draw different birds in this way, ones with chubby chests like robins and long necks like swans.

You can draw fish using the same types of curves, but this time draw the curves of the two lines running against one another. To obtain a long, thin fish such as a mackerel, draw gentle, long curves; for a flat-looking fish such as a plaice, use deep curves. Add any details as appropriate.

Make the templates, adding seam allowances if necessary. Cut out the fabric and apply to the base fabric using the appropriate method. You can add details of feathers, tails, fins and eyes later. You could make eyes from circles of fabric gathered up around the edge, flattened and then applied to the bird or fish with the gathering underneath, giving a three-dimensional look to the eye.

Look for special fabrics, shiny or with small repeat patterns, which would represent the scales of the fish. You could also add sequins to give sparkle, or embroidery for the detail of the scales, once you have applied the shapes to the base fabric.

Birds and fish drawn with simple curving lines

A landscape of birds and fish

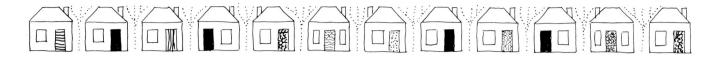

Houses

A building is often used as a central feature of a quilt. This could be pieced, stencilled, cut out in one piece or made up of a series of different pieces and applied. Design the house as a whole to begin with, whichever way you intend to make it. Do not try to put every feature of the house into the design: list the main features, and select those which give the building its character. Perspective can be difficult, so simplify this aspect.

Draw a rectangle in the correct proportion to fit the house. Divide it up horizontally to represent the levels of the house, and vertically to represent the upright divisions such as the doorway, window positions or any other features. Now try to draw the house you want on this grid in outline, using the lines of the grid and the diagonals of the grid sections as actual lines. Then draw in the windows and doorway, and adjust any of the lines to capture the exact character you require. Think of the rectangles and square shapes as building bricks.

Now decide if you want to apply this shape in one piece or as individual pieces. If you apply it in one piece, you will need a template showing all the shapes of the windows, doors and other features. These could be worked in reverse appliqué (see page 24). If the house is to be applied in a group of pieces, make templates for all the individual pieces, adding seam allowances if necessary, and work out the order in which to apply them. For instance, the roof might best be applied over the walls, but the windows might be best treated as if they were underneath the walls, giving the feeling that they open into a space. This will mean that the template for the walls will need to have the windows cut out. Carry out some trials in coloured paper to work out exactly how you will order the work.

If you wish to show perspective because without it the house will just not look right, try to work out the shape using triangles, as is shown in the drawing below of the house with a side extension and bay windows.

Details of flowers, birds, butterflies and any other delights of a garden may be applied as extras or embroidered. The use of an unrealistic scale is perhaps something that could be used to advantage where a feeling of space is required in a small area.

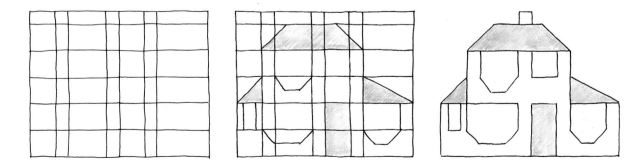

How to draw a house with the help of a grid

Streets of houses

Two very different styles of embroidery used for naming a quilt

6
The quilt is finished

An appliqué quilt will have taken a long time to complete, perhaps several years, especially if most of the work was done by hand. I started to plan *Rondo* about four years before finishing it. This is a great period in one's life, and inevitably the quilt becomes almost a way of life. There is much satisfaction in completing a quilt, so take time to admire it, photograph it and derive pleasure from a task well done. This will help to alleviate the empty feeling that sets in on its completion.

Record the history of the quilt for generations to come, because something that has taken so long to make is worth recording. Give the quilt a name and date it. Spend time putting the basic points on the quilt, together with your name as the maker. This can be done in a variety of ways, either on the front or the back of the quilt, and can even be thought out at the planning stage and incorporated in the design. The labelling need not be intrusive on the design: it can be embroidered in cross-stitch or another equally suitable stitch, written with a laundry marker, or even machine-embroidered. Some of the modern sewing machines have letters and numbers in their working programme which makes labelling quite simple. I have seen all these methods used with equal success. I personally use my machine to draw the label on a separate piece of calico and then sew it on to the back of the quilt. You can see two different quilt labellings in the photographs shown opposite.

The quilt is worth keeping safe, so take precautions to store it away from direct light, animals and dirt. The best way to store it is flat on a bed, and if not in general use upside-down, turning it over of course for visitors. Another way to store a quilt is to roll it, face outward, between two sheets on a tube. If there is no space for this, the quilt will have to be folded. Place it face down on a clean sheet with another on top and then fold them up together. This will prevent severe creasing. It is a good idea to re-fold the quilt in a different way frequently.

If the quilt is to be hung on a wall, avoid a position which has direct sunlight on it or any draughts that will produce dust. Give the quilt a gentle vacuum clean periodically with an upholstery nozzle covered over with a piece of net or nylon stocking to protect the quilt surface.

If you have enjoyed making this quilt then you will already have another one in mind to make. Be more adventurous for the next one, and use what you have learned from this quilt. Collect new source ideas, start to assemble fabrics, looking for the unusual, and plan well ahead.

Jewel flowers quilt by Joan Fogg from an original design source of carpets and rugs

(Opposite) Quilt by Jean Powell showing her own personal and unusual style of appliqué using embroidery to outline the shapes

FURTHER READING

Ashley, Clifford W. *The Ashley Book of Knots* (Faber and Faber)

Bain, Iain *Celtic Knotwork* (Constable)

Bawden, Juliet *The Art and Craft of Appliqué* (Mitchell Beazley)

Bewes, Peter and Mathey, Francis *Animals in Art* (Odhams Books, Hamlyn)

Carter, David *Butterflies and Moths in Britain and Europe* (Pan)

Dance, S. Peter *The Hamlyn Guide to Shells of the World* (Hamlyn)

Hayden, Ruth *Mrs Delany and her Flower Collages* (British Museum Publications)

Hillier, Malcolm and Hilton, Colin *The Complete Book of Dried Flowers* (Dorling Kindersley)

Keeble Martin, W. *The Concise British Flora in Colour* (Sphere)

Linsell, Keith and Pritchard, Michael *Fresh and Saltwater Fish* (HarperCollins)

Manners, Errol *Ceramics Source Book* (Quarto)

Osler, Dorothy *Quilting* (Merehurst)

Ribeiro, Aileen and Cummings, Valerie *The Visual History of Costume* (Batsford)

Rice, Matthew *Village Buildings of Britain* (Little, Brown)

Seward, Linda *The Complete Book of Patchwork, Quilting and Appliqué* (Mitchell Beazley)

The Book of British Birds (Drive Publications)

The Field Guide to the Animals of Britain (Readers Digest)

Travis, Dinah *The Sampler Quilt Workbook* (Batsford)

Vedel, Helge and Lange, Johan *Trees and Bushes in Wood and Hedgerow* (Methuen)

USEFUL ADDRESSES

Societies

American Quilters' Society
PO Box 3290
Paducah
Kentucky 42002-3290
USA

The Quilters' Guild
OP66 Dean Clough
Halifax
West Yorkshire HX3 5AX
UK

For fabrics

Laura Ashley Ltd
PO Box 19
Newtown
Powys SY16 1DZ
UK

Liberty Retail Ltd
Regent Street
London W1R 6AH
UK

Piecemakers
13 Manor Green Road
Epsom
Surrey KT19 8RA
UK

Strawberry Fayre
(Mail order only)
Chagford
Devon TQ13 8EN
UK

The Quilt Room
20 West Street
Dorking
Surrey RH4 1BL
UK

Village Fabrics
Lester Way
Wallingford
Oxfordshire OX10 9DD
UK

INDEX